WHEN PARENTS WORRY

WHEN PARENTS WORRY

The Real Calls Doctors Receive ... from Moles
That Seem to Move to Funny-Smelling Poo

HENRY ANDERSON, MD

Avon, Massachusetts

Published by
Adams Media, a division of F+W Media, Inc.
57 Littlefield Street, Avon, MA 02322.
U.S.A.
www.adamsmedia.com

ISBN 10: 1-4405-4548-0
ISBN 13: 978-1-4405-4548-1
eISBN 10: 1-4405-4549-9
eISBN 13: 978-1-4405-4549-8

Printed in the United States of America.

10   9   8   7   6   5   4   3   2   1

Library of Congress Cataloging-in-Publication Data

Anderson, Henry.
  When parents worry / Henry Anderson.
     p. cm.
  ISBN 978-1-4405-4548-1 (pbk.) – ISBN 1-4405-4548-0 (pbk.) – ISBN 978-1-4405-4549-8 (ebook) – ISBN 1-4405-4549-9 (ebook)
1. Parenting–Humor. 2. Physicians–Humor. 3. Sick children–Humor. I. Title.
  PN6231.P2A53 2012
  818'.607–dc23

2012023730

This book is available at quantity discounts for bulk purchases.
For information, please call 1-800-289-0963.

Introduction

If there's one thing I know for certain, it's that children do not come with instruction manuals. As a pediatrician, I've seen it all—kids stuffing M&M's up their noses, kissing live frogs, and even drinking toilet water. Nothing can compare to some of the things I've heard from sleep-deprived parents with the best intentions.

Over the years, I've received hundreds of distressed phone calls from well-meaning moms and dads concerned about everything from their child's eating habits to the risks of sitting on Santa's lap. Sure, sometimes their concerns and requests are a little bizarre, baffling even, but then again, so is the wild adventure we call parenthood. This book celebrates that chaotic world of stomachaches, bumps and bruises, and unnecessary pangs of worry with real phone messages from concerned parents whose kid just . . .

Our one-month-old likes to watch *Gilligan's Island* reruns during her 4:30 A.M. feeding. Is that okay?

I was changing my child's diaper, and
he peed in his own eye. I'm panicking.
Is he going to go blind?

 A toilet bowl lid fell on
our son's penis.
Please call when you get
a chance.

I have a question regarding which
mattress to buy for Harry. Please call
because the sale is ending today.

We're concerned because our three-year-old son Mikey is getting excited about girls.

I left my grocery list in your office at my visit an hour ago, and now I don't know what to buy at the store.

 My daughter has become a real monster. Do you think that the "threes" have become the new "twos"?

My cat has cancer and I'm worried it's contagious, especially if Jane swallows some of the cat's hair.

The school nurse keeps sending our son home and saying he's sick. We told her that he saw the doctor and everything's fine, but we didn't really come in to the office. Now she wants a note from you. What should we do?

 My son has a cough. Can I put Vicks VapoRub on his feet and cover them with socks?

My son sucks his thumb so much, I think it's falling off.

My son was seen in your office for a cold. I need a note stating that he can return to swim class.
(This call was received on December 22nd . . . I saw him on November 28th.)

My son has been biting some kids in preschool. Do you think he'll be violent later in life?

Vicky's shoulder has been hurting after she plays Wii.

My husband wants to take our three-year-old daughter skiing. I don't think it's safe. Who's right?

 I'm concerned because Jane's foot hasn't grown in a year.

I would like to see a chiropractor because our three-month-old is colicky. Do you have any recommendations?

Bobby's vitamins are making him hyper. Is there anything we can do?

 My child was running around a lot, and now her heart is beating really fast.

My one-year-old can't say, "Mama." Instead, she calls me "Dada." Is that a problem?

Is it okay if we switch between regular and organic milk?

 My nine-year-old daughter has been having headaches for two weeks. She fell out of a shopping cart at Home Depot when she was three years old. Do you think that's causing her headaches?

My son is a very poor sleeper and wakes up really easily. My husband is so scared that he'll wake him up at night that he's been peeing in a mayonnaise jar in our bedroom instead of going out into the hallway to go to the bathroom. Please, please help us.

Our ten-year-old son saw an inappropriate film about sex on the Internet. Is there an appropriate sex video we could show him?

My daughter likes her milk cold. Must we heat it up?

Sometimes when my baby cries, no sound comes out. Is that okay?

My son is always a bit hyper, but now that he is on antibiotics, he is significantly nuttier than usual. What should I do?

 Should my eight-year-old wear boxers or briefs?

Rebecca complains that her hands hurt, but only when we ask her to brush her teeth. What do you think?

My one-year-old sleeps thirteen hours overnight and takes two naps of two hours every day. Shouldn't she have more of a life?

I noticed that the tips of my son's ears are yellow. What does that mean?

Can my two-month-old sit on Santa's lap for a photo?

 My eight-month-old ate her first banana yesterday. Today, she has a fever. Do you think the banana gave her a fever?

My seven-day-old has been eating nonstop, and I can't seem to stop feeding him. Is it okay if I stop?

My daughter stuck the wand from her Nintendo up my son's nose. I'm worried it punctured his brain. Please call.

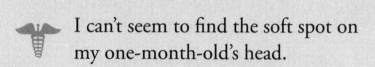 I can't seem to find the soft spot on my one-month-old's head.

Johnny is tall. Is he too tall?
(The child is six months old.)

Are you still seeing new patients? I know you're a pediatrician, but this one time, can you examine my puppy?

Arlene fell while playing in the snow yesterday. Her birthday party is in five days. How will the black-and-blue mark on her face look by then?

My mother said
my son has a
skinny penis.
Please call ASAP.

I want to get my son excused from gym class due to asthma so that he can take Driver's Ed.

I'm bringing my three-month-old to a White Sox game today, and I was wondering if you think the noise might be too much for him.

My daughter Jane is five months old, and she keeps rolling over onto her belly in her sleep. I keep rolling her back as often as I can, but I'm worried about the middle of the night. What can I do?

 Mark is on his fifth day of antibiotics for strep throat. Can he go bicycle riding?

My son took two of my husband's Viagra pills. Will this hurt him?

My daughter Claire has a bad rash, but I don't want to come in to the office. Can I describe it over the phone so you can tell me what it is?

I'm breastfeeding and I ate a pretzel made with honey. Is that okay? Because I know babies aren't supposed to eat honey.

Mikey just started to walk, and he keeps falling down. I'm worried that he's in danger. Please advise.

My son stuck an M&M up his nose. Do we need to get it out, or will it just melt away?

Mark swam in a swimming pool yesterday where they found a dead frog. We're concerned. Please call.

Renee is napping with her arm under her body, and now it looks a bit blue. She's still asleep. Do you think we should move her arm?

A sewer pipe burst in my basement, and I had to wade through the slime to clean it up. Can I still breastfeed?

 When I'm feeding my baby, does a fart equal a burp?

A bird pooped in my daughter's mouth yesterday. Do we need to worry about anything?

My two-year-old daughter ate the wax covering on her Baby Bell cheese. I'm not sure if this is a problem. Can you please call?

 Bobby is complaining of lower back pain. It all started when he did "the worm" in school today. Please call and tell us what we should do.

Can you tell me what should be a normal day for a one-month-old?

My newborn's poop smells like buttered popcorn. What should we do?

 I would like a note stating that my son has problems with frequent urination so that he can be changed to a nicer kindergarten classroom, which, by the way, has a potty present.

When my daughter pees, the water in the toilet splashes up. Do you think it could cause a urinary tract infection?

About a month ago, Stacey ate some stale cereal. Now she has had extra smelly poop for the last week. Do you think they're related?

We are going away to a remote Greek island for two weeks. What should we do if we get sick or something?

Our dog sat on our child's nose
a few months ago, and now it has
a bump. How can you tell if it's
broken?

Please call. Steven took poop out
of his diaper. We're not sure if he
ate any.

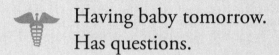 Having baby tomorrow.
Has questions.

My daughter bumped her head on
the toilet when she bent down to
pull up her pants. Now she has a
big lump on her forehead. Please
call to advise.

I need a note stating my son doesn't have to go outside for recess on freezing days.

 My daughter's stool is very green. I think she may have swallowed a crayon, though I'm not sure. Please call to advise.

My son Steven was on the toilet last night after my nanny had cleaned it. Some of the blue water in the bowl splashed up and hit his behind, and he said it burned. Will there be any long-term effects?

 Sarah has pubic hair in her underarms. Can we shave it?

My daughter bobs her head in her high chair while she's listening to rap music. Please call.

My son has been eating dog food—whole handfuls—out of the dog's bowl. Should we ignore it and hope he stops?

Tina just finished playing soccer and now her foot hurts. Should we bring her in?

My three-month-old slept through the night last night. What should I do?

 My son's testicle is breathing. It's kind of moving in and out.

Brian pooped corn. Is that normal?

 Peter is four years old, and he might have been bitten by a dog. I'm just not sure it happened, because the only witness was Tracey, his thirteen-month-old sister.

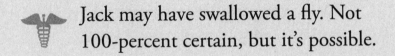 Jack may have swallowed a fly. Not 100-percent certain, but it's possible.

Is it okay for Danny to be at the beach for two hours?

When my eighteen-month-old reads a book, she holds it upside down and too close to her face. Do you think she has a learning disability?

Can my ten-year-old son drink coffee?

Donna pooped in the bathtub last week, and now she won't take a bath anymore.

When my son woke up in the middle of the night, he seemed a little incoherent. His father thinks he has issues, but I think he was half asleep. Please call to tell us who is right.

 Our dog jumped onto my son's stomach. Please call because I'm concerned about internal bleeding.

Frank is fourteen years old and needs a personal trainer. Do you have any recommendations?

My son Carl is supposed to be on an asthma inhaler. It says on the label that he's supposed to take it daily, but he hasn't in months. Is he supposed to? I thought you might know.

Betty ate cheese from a mousetrap from which the mouse also ate. Is that anything to worry about?

Rachel sat on a less-than-clean toilet seat in a public bathroom. Is she going to get an infection?

 I don't know how to say this, but I'm worried my son's "member" may be too big.

Leslie, our seven-year-old, wants to give up taking karate. Can you please explain to her how important it is that she continues?

 Michelle has something blue in her ear.
(It was ice cream sprinkles.)

Myra has had a Band-Aid on her face for three days. We took it off and now the area looks red and puffy.

We are going to a Rolling Stones concert. How can we protect our three-month-old's ears?

A chipmunk fell out of a tree and landed on my daughter's head. Can you check the scratches she got?

My three-year-old ate a donut with mold on it.

We went to see fireworks yesterday with Leon, our six-month-old. Now he's acting weird. He keeps laughing when he sees things falling.

My daughter
has a mole,
which—I'm pretty
sure—moved to
a different spot.
Please call to
advise.

We have five cats and two dogs. My six-month-old has a runny nose. Could it be allergies?

Whenever my son eats a pickle, his poop looks like a pickle. Is that abnormal?

Mark ate an M&M that was a few years old. Need advice ASAP.

Sydney's pacifier fell out of her mouth while we were shopping at Walmart. I accidentally put it back in her mouth without washing it. What should I watch for?

I'm worried that my son's weightlifting could stunt his growth. He is six-foot-two, but he could be six-foot-four.

My five-year-old is getting re-circumcised on Friday. How should I tell him?

My child is on amoxicillin, and since he began the medication his poop doesn't smell.

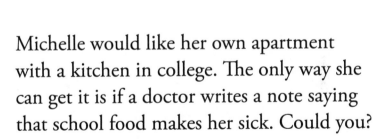

Rachel was in the office yesterday for a viral illness, and today she can't stop burping.

Michelle would like her own apartment with a kitchen in college. The only way she can get it is if a doctor writes a note saying that school food makes her sick. Could you?

My son's testicles disappeared.

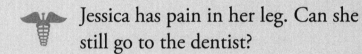 Jessica has pain in her leg. Can she still go to the dentist?

My son has had belly pain for three days. Can we have a note to get him out of traffic court?

(A call that was received at 4:45 A.M.) My two-month-old daughter didn't sleep well during the day. Now she has been sleeping for seven hours. What should we do?

I would like to discuss our potential babysitter's qualifications.

 When my son Bart watches TV, he tilts his head to the side. Is there something wrong with him?

I think my son stuck a button up his nose three months ago. We never found it, but now he keeps picking his nose.

My son has a 104°F fever, but I want to send him to school to keep his mind off his illness. What do you think?

Can my three-week-old go to Atlantic City for the weekend?
(I told them yes, but no Blackjack.)

My son bit another boy. The school nurse said that he needs to see the doctor. Isn't it usually the child who gets bitten who needs to be seen?

My son keeps complaining his penis is hard.

My husband wants to buy a Porsche. I'm concerned about the risk of whiplash for our son. Please call. (Apparently, the mother was trying to use this as leverage to talk her husband out of buying a sports car.)

 Can my six-year-old run a five-kilometer race with me?

My thirteen-year-old
daughter is very emotional.

My baby fell out of her crib
last night. Now I'm at Sleepy's
shopping for a toddler bed.
Which one should I get?

 Allen started sleeping through
the night. Now he's missing
two feedings.

I would like to discuss my daughter's parent-teacher conference with you.

 Sometimes my son's stool looks like a baked potato.

Can you please listen to my eleven-year-old cough into the phone so that you can tell why he's coughing?

Can we use Scope to get the white stuff off our one-month-old's tongue?

My son used to hiccup all the time, now not as much. Is that okay?

Can we get a testosterone level on our fifteen-year-old? Because he's not so interested in girls.

My daughter is sitting on the toilet with a bowel movement half stuck. Please call soon.

 My child has ongoing Irrational Bowel Syndrome.

Frank is one week old, and he won't pee when he has a diaper on.

My daughter is three days old, and she has a temperature of 98.6°F.

My son was seen yesterday for wrist pain. Today, it still hurts after he shoveled the snow.

 My daughter has a 10 A.M. appointment, which I need to cancel because she's cranky. (The patient is sixteen years old.)

Nicholas is sick, and I need him well because he's missing camp and it's $150 a day.

My babysitter put Tylenol in my son's ears instead of eardrops. Please call.

My daughter really likes kidney beans. I have been giving them to her a lot, and now she has had loose stools for a few days and wakes up crying.

My daughter's rear end is on fire and it's spreading. Please call to advise.

My two-and-a-half-year-old son keeps saying he's a girl. Should he know that he's a boy?

My husband awoke with stomach cramps. I know you're a pediatrician, but couldn't you just see him this one time?

Wax comes out of my son's ear when he blows his nose.

I'm going on a cruise with my children. Should we take anything with us?

 My daughter has been constipated—but only on Fridays—for the last few weeks.

You told me to call if my newborn vomits any feedings after we get home from the hospital. She did.

My baby just ate the crinkly paper attached to her play mat.
Please advise.

My daughter was constipated for days. I gave her an enema and now she has diarrhea.

(A call that was received on Labor Day)
My son is fine, but I just want him checked out before school starts.

My daughter Regina came home from school and has vomited twice in the past hour. I'm in Paris, but my nanny is at home with Regina. Please call to advise her, but speak slowly, as she doesn't speak English.

 We would like to bring Veronica into the office so that you can watch her eat peanut butter for the first time and make sure she's okay.

My eighteen-month-old has black ink on his hands. How do you remove it?

My son has a lump in his neck that moves by itself. Is this a problem?

Our Gymboree teacher feels Ray has poor upper arm strength.

My daughter was diagnosed with strep two days ago. I need a note stating she can sing a solo in her school play.

 I accidentally refrigerated a medication that didn't require refrigeration. Please call to advise.

We're going to Colorado with our son, to an altitude of 8,000 feet. What should we do?

My son has an ear infection. My friend said she cured her son's infection by blowing a hair dryer in his ears. What's your opinion?

Can you find us a new allergist? Our old one was arrested on child pornography charges.

My fifteen-month-old will only use her sippy cup and refuses to use her bottle anymore. What should we do?

We were in the office today because my daughter had stomach cramps. We just gave her a suppository, and a nickel and a dime came out. Please call as soon as possible.

My child wore a Halloween mask today, and now his face is swollen.

My son was given a very strong hug. I'm very concerned.

 I'm bringing in a thorn bush attached to our daughter's hand.

The school nurse keeps sending my daughter home because she's sick. She's not.

My son has a red mark on his hands from hanging from the monkey bars. Please advise.

My one-year-old son slept for three hours in daycare two days in a row. With my background in psychology, I thought he might be depressed.

I'm not sure if Jeremy ate a glycerin suppository or if he was using it as ChapStick. Do I need to call poison control?

My three-month-old is sleeping through the night. Is that okay?

 My fifteen-year-old got a tongue ring without our permission. We made him take it out, but he keeps putting it back in. Please call to advise.

I'm pregnant and I'm thinking of breastfeeding, but I'm worried my baby won't get some of the benefits of formula.

Is it okay for my eight-month-old to stand, or will she get bow-legged?

For the past two years, when my child eats spicy food, her left ear hurts.

My child's toes are turning green.

My son is dating a girl with shingles. Should he break up with her?

Can you please check Jimmy's ears? Because he's afraid of the wind.

Can my son have a goose as a pet?

 We're in Texas on vacation. Can my five-month-old son drink water so that he doesn't get dehydrated?

My kid is possessed by some sort of gas devil.

My daughter's rectum is tingly. It only stops when she pinches her cheeks together.

My daughter was in the office this morning and was diagnosed with strep. She has bad belly pain. She won't eat anything but pizza bagels, and the pain isn't going away.

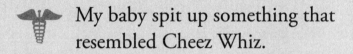 My baby spit up something that resembled Cheez Whiz.

How much weight do you think my son will lose after his circumcision?

Are sound soothers addictive?

My son keeps lifting one of his arms higher than the other.

 My son heard someone say the four-letter curse word starting with an "s," and now he won't stop saying it. What should we do?

What is the medical term for when a baby gets around by moving on his behind? My daughter is writing an essay for school.

When we give our two-week-old a sponge bath, can we sponge her face and forehead?

Can I take my child to the zoo?

One of my twins swallowed a
penny, but I'm not sure which
one it was.

My child is very starchy.

 My child has a white head
on his penis.

My three-year-old was eating ice cream, and he bit off and swallowed part of the plastic spoon. What should I do?

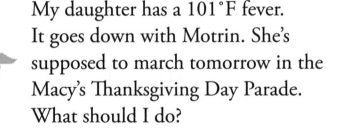

My daughter has a 101°F fever. It goes down with Motrin. She's supposed to march tomorrow in the Macy's Thanksgiving Day Parade. What should I do?

I am concerned that some of my son's sickness is a ploy to stay home from preschool. I'm not sure if he is that smart, but whatever your diagnosis, please tell him that school is important and he needs to go and learn.
(He had an ear infection.)

My daughter screams when we get in the car. What should I do?

My son's penis is weird. It looks like it's hiding.

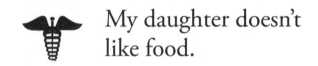 My daughter doesn't like food.

I need a note to change my daughter's lunch period. It's too late in the day because she doesn't eat breakfast.

We called 911 last night because my son had very, very bad constipation. He passed the stool before the ambulance arrived, but we need to discuss it with you.

I am due to have a baby in a few weeks. My sister has diarrhea now. Can she see the baby when it's born?

I am painting and carpeting our new nursery. Can you please advise us on what to buy?

 Can my four-month-old go to see fireworks? Also, he accidentally drank whole milk.

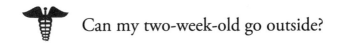 Can my two-week-old go outside?

My daughter ate her brother's poop.

 My daughter was playing in snow.
Now her feet are red and tingly.

.

My son is four years old now.
Can we stop using Dreft on his
laundry?

My son's nose is a different
color than his face.

 My son is going on a play date with
someone who has had pneumonia
and an ear infection since
Wednesday. Is this okay? It's a very
important play date.

Diaper is dry.
Blanket is soaked.
Please advise.

My child licked a black marker off the table, and now his whole mouth is black. Can you tell us how to get it off?

How can we tell if our baby is hot or cold?

 Can you please tell me the adult dose for liquid Tylenol?

Our three-week-old has been forming little drool mouth bubbles. Is that okay?

We found our two-year-old in the kitchen with an open bottle of beer, but we're not sure how much she drank. Can you give us a call?

My daughter Ricki has become so independent that if we wipe food off her face after she eats, she has a tantrum unless we put the food back on so she can wipe it off herself. Do we really need to do that?

My son's socks make a mark on his legs when he wears them. Is that okay?

Now that my daughter has had the chicken pox, can she eat chicken?

 My daughter's nails haven't grown in the last month. Normally, I would have had to trim them by now. Please give us a call.

Our fifteen-month-old keeps falling when she walks. My friend suggested she has "gravitational insecurity." What do you think?

 So many of our friends' kids are receiving occupational therapy or physical therapy. My son is very coordinated, but could there be any reason he needs it?

How should I prepare my ten-month-old's meat?

 The thermometer says 98°F, but I know it's not right. What should we do?

My eighteen-year-old does not want to get a flu shot. Please text her to tell her she needs it.

My son will eat Beefaroni and nothing else. Is that a problem?

We just bought our daughter a sippy cup. What should we put in it?

 We skipped a week of vitamins. What should we do now?

My son stuck a BB pellet in his ear, but the emergency room doctor checked and said it's not there anymore. Could it have fallen into his brain?

What is the scientific term for boogers?

 I have two mothers-in-law (my father-in-law remarried—can you imagine?). One said one thing about feeding, and the other said the opposite. Can you break the tie?

It's early April, but it's really warm outside. Can my son start wearing shorts?

My mother told my four-year-old daughter that her belly is big, and now she's become paranoid about her belly. Please explain to her that it's a nice belly.

My son is humping everything and he will not stop. Please call to advise.

My son went on a roller coaster and now he's very pale. Please call when you get a chance.

 How long should we wait before we have another child?

Would mosquito netting be effective in preventing the flu?

Michael ate a bologna sandwich that was three days old, but he didn't vomit. Naturally, we're concerned. Please call.

My fourteen-month-old has a cold, but we're due to have another baby this week and don't want to come in if you're not going to give us any medication.

My six-month-old has a cold. My Russian mother-in-law suggested I rub vodka on her chest. What do you think?

The area around my daughter's mouth smells like cauliflower. Please call to advise.

The prescription from the pharmacy said to give the antibiotics for my daughter's ear infection vaginally. Is that correct?

My daughter Jane mistook some cat feces for a pretzel. What should we do?

My son was playing out in the snow for a long time and now his cheeks are red. Could it be frostbite?

 I was dancing with my fifteen-year-old son and he asked to be dipped. Now his neck hurts.

The eye doctor says my daughter passed her eye exam, but she wants glasses because her brother has them. What should I do?

My son had a test for tuberculosis two weeks ago, and now he has diarrhea. Please call to advise.

When I hug my daughter, I hear a humming sound.

My two-year-old shoved a banana up her nose. Is it important to get it out, or will it work its way out eventually?

My child just put a frog on his tongue.

 Every time my son pushes on his nose, he vomits up mucus. Please call to advise.

My son has a cold. Which tea would help him get better faster: fennel or chamomile?

 My daughter Joan failed her eye exam at the ophthalmologist. I want a second opinion.

My nine-month-old laughs hysterically sometimes.
Please call.

My daughter has a cold sore in her mouth and numbness of the second toe on her left foot.

We have a few questions for you regarding our five-month-old because we haven't seen you in a few weeks. Can we take him to Vegas?

I dropped off my son's urine sample in a Tupperware container. Can you please give it back when you're done?

 My son's scrotum got caught in a spring-loaded keychain. What do we do now?

We want to introduce new foods to our baby. When can we start with caviar?

My two-month-
old is drooling a
lot. Do you think
she's imitating
our dog?

Dr. Oz said my son's poop should be soft and shaped like a question mark, but it's actually kind of hard and looks like a semicolon. Any thoughts?

My child's diarrhea is a weird shade of green. Can I email you a picture?

 Should our four-year-old have an iPad?

You said I should give my son mineral oil for his constipation. I found an old bottle of it around the house that I used to use on the furniture. Can I use that?

My daughter Erin is eight weeks old. My husband started vomiting yesterday. I think he has stomach flu. Do you think he should move out of the house until he's better, or should we move out?

My son wore thrift-shop pants yesterday, and now he has an itchy rash on his legs. Do you think it's related?

Is it okay for Danny to join a soccer team? There's a lot of bouncing the ball on your head.

It's too ugly outside for me to go out and buy my daughter cold medicine. Can we give her chicken soup instead?

 My child ate stickers and coughed some out. Help!

I think my daughter's having night terrors. She's kind of flying out of her crib.

My daughter was exposed to someone who was exposed to the flu. What should I do?

I think my three-year-old daughter has an ear infection, but she's refusing to go to the doctor.

My teenage daughter swallowed her tongue ring. What should we do?

Elizabeth was bit by a donkey at the petting zoo. Please call.

 Can you remind me of the name of the cream you prescribed? All I remember was that it was for acne and it was expensive.

Can you give me the name of a good hypnotist?

 My daughter usually has three bowel movements a day, and today she had only two. Please call when you get a chance.

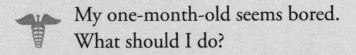 My one-month-old seems bored.
What should I do?

My nine-month-old only likes to
play with red toys. Do you think
there's something wrong with him?

I have a nutrition question. As a snack, how many Twinkies are too many?

Can my five-year-old use our treadmill to exercise?

 My ten-month-old is scared of bald people. It probably wouldn't be such a big deal, but her grandfather is "follicly challenged."

We're on vacation and our daughter was stung by a Portuguese man-of-war. Do we need to pee on her?

 When we were in the office yesterday, you said Sheryl should be better by Sunday. Will that be in the morning or the afternoon, because she has an audition?

When my daughter threw up today, I noticed grass in the vomit. I'm worried that she and her friends might be grazing. Please call.

My daughter picked her nose and then ate a cookie with her own booger on it. Is she going to get sick?

My daughter's underarm smell is beyond B.O. Any suggestions?

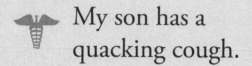 My son has a quacking cough.

My son is growing so quickly. I bought him pants on Friday, and they were too short by Monday. Is that normal?

My son smells like he has a fever. Should I give him Tylenol?

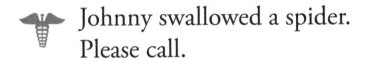 Johnny swallowed a spider. Please call.

When my son sneezes, he pinches his nose so that the boogers don't go flying out all over the place. I'm worried that causes too much pressure in his head. Is that going to hurt his brain?

My son's seasonal allergies are getting worse. Could you please drug him up and make him better?

Janey gets a cold every time she sleeps on her right side. It happens a lot. Is that normal?

What should I do
when my son goes
boneless?